MW00711576

To our precious children—
Rob, Claire, Brittnye, and Ashley

To Bridget
Love, Cindy

Photo Credits include: Roy Gumpel/TSI–page 7; Stewart Cohen/TSI–page 25; Dan Bosler/TSI–page 35; From *A Week in the Life of the LCMS*–page 15; Cleo Photography–page 43.

1 2 3 4 5 6 7 8 9 10   08 07 06 05 04 03 02 01 00 99

THE
ABC's
of
CHRISTIAN
Mothers
AND
DAUGHTERS

Twenty-six ways to love and nurture
your daughter today and every day

Robert & Debra Bruce

CPH
Concordia Publishing House

Accept

your daughter unconditionally

as a gift from your heavenly Father.

Learn to find rays of hope—even

in seemingly hopeless situations.

Dear children, let us not love with words
or tongue but with actions and in truth.

1 John 3:18

Break

the habit of giving in to your

daughter's every demand—

and do so positively. Help her to

become self-reliant so she learns to

take care of her own needs creatively.

He cuts off every branch in me that bears
no fruit, while every branch that does
bear fruit He prunes so that it will be
even more fruitful.

John 15:2

Communicate

caring through touch.

A pat on the shoulder, a warm hug,

or cuddling while watching TV can

generate a stronger sense of caring

and concern than spoken words.

He tends His flock like a shepherd:
He gathers the lambs in His arms and
carries them close to His heart; and He
gently leads those that have young.

Isaiah 40:11

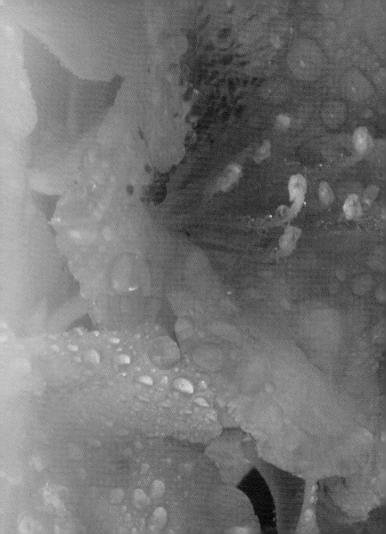

*O*rop your parenting guard once in awhile.

Structure your home for discipline,

but remember that it is a place for

celebration, laughter, and fellowship.

Bring the fattened calf and kill it.
Let's have a feast and celebrate.
For this son of mine was dead
and is alive again; he was lost and is found.
So they began to celebrate.

Luke 15:23–24

Evaluate

your parenting attitude from time

to time, keeping in mind that your

expectations and attitude—

no matter how positive or negative—

greatly influence the path your

daughter will take.

This is what the Sovereign LORD, the Holy One of Israel, says: "In repentance and rest is your salvation, in quietness and trust is your strength."

Isaiah 30:15

Follow

the perfect example of Jesus Christ

in your life. He patiently listened

to each person, empathized with the

problems at hand, and shared *agape*

or selfless love while sending

a positive message of God's love.

Therefore, since we have been justified
through faith, we have peace with God
through our Lord Jesus Christ.   *Romans 5:1*

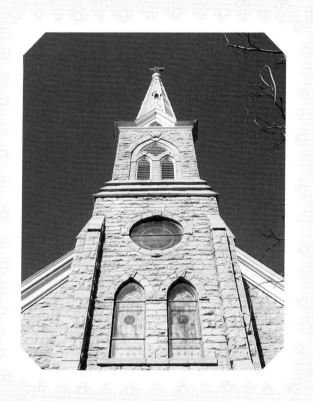

Get

off any negative track

with your daughter. Chart a new,

positive course in Christian living,

letting go of past failures and mistakes

—both yours and hers.

Brothers, I do not consider myself yet to have
taken hold of it. But one thing I do: Forgetting
what is behind and straining toward what is
ahead, I press on toward the goal to win the
prize for which God has called me heavenward
in Christ Jesus.   *Philippians 3:13–14*

Help

her view life's hurdles

with ultimate hope and optimism,

and encourage her to become

the best she can, striving

for eternal rewards.

May the God of hope fill you with all joy
and peace as you trust in Him,
so that you may overflow with hope
by the power of the Holy Spirit.

Romans 15:13

Identify

attempts by your daughter to manipulate you through anger or peer pressure. When she says, "everyone else gets to," talk openly about your family's values and present a united front as you hold fast to your rules.

I appeal to you, brothers, in the name of our Lord Jesus Christ, that all of you agree with one another so that there may be no divisions among you and that you be perfectly united in mind and thought.   *1 Corinthians 1:10*

Just as you carefully choose what you eat, read, or whom you imitate, guide your daughter in selecting quality programs on television. Talk openly about opposing values depicted on TV, and discuss how Christians are different.

Command and teach these things. Don't let anyone look down on you because you are young, but set an example for the believers in speech, in life, in love, in faith and in purity.

1 Timothy 4:11–12

$\mathcal{K}$now

when to seek help from others.

Call your pastor, doctor, or other

professional if you have a concern

about your daughter that is creating

havoc in the family.

Is any one of you sick? He should call the
elders of the church to pray over him and
anoint him with oil in the name of the Lord.

James 5:14

Lay

a positive foundation

for your daughter, teaching her

ways to care and show empathy

to family and friends.

If anyone has material possessions and
sees his brother in need but has no pity
on him, how can the love of God be in him?
1 John 3:17

Modify

the worry habit; replace it

with prayer, outreach, and positive

thinking. Teach your daughter to let

go of persistent worries, turning

them over to God.

Cast all your anxiety on Him because
He cares for you.

1 Peter 5:7

Nurture

personal growth as you make

time to affirm your daughter.

Model positive biblical absolutes.

If you obey My commands, you will remain
in My love, just as I have obeyed My Father's
commands and remain in His love.

John 15:10

Offer

respect, forgiveness, affection,

and acceptance. The best way

for your daughter to learn these

Christian attributes is for you

to model them.

Bear with each other and forgive whatever
grievances you may have against one
another. Forgive as the Lord forgave you.

Colossians 3:13

Pray

consistently each day

with your daughter. Share answers

to prayer, and talk about God's

master plan for her life.

But when you pray, go into your room,
close the door and pray to your Father,
who is unseen. Then your Father, who sees
what is done in secret, will reward you.

Matthew 6:6

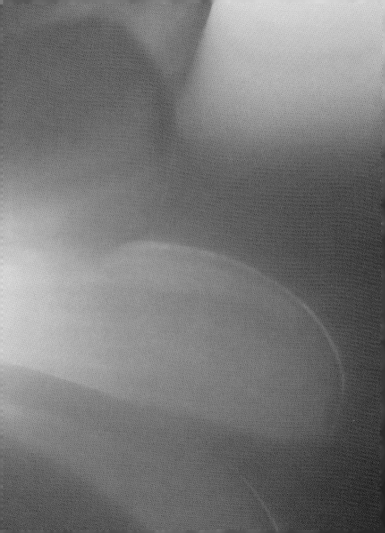

Quit

trying to be perfect!

Teach your daughter that as

human beings, we are imperfect.

As children of God, we can enjoy

God's grace at work in us to bring

us to wholeness and completion.

I always thank God for you because
of His grace given you in Christ Jesus.

1 Corinthians 1:4

Remember,

sometimes actions count more than

words. Thoughts, feelings,

and behavior mirror the soul, but

your spoken words can tear down or

build up your daughter.

Let your conversation be always full
of grace, seasoned with salt, so that you
may know how to answer everyone.
Colossians 4:6

Say,

"I'm sorry" when you are wrong.

Verbal acknowledgment of wrong-

doing is essential to a positive

mother-daughter relationship.

Therefore, if you are offering your gift
at the altar and there remember that your
brother has something against you,
leave your gift there in front of the altar.
First go and be reconciled to your brother;
then come and offer your gift.

Matthew 5:23–24

_J_ell

her stories from your own life

that give relief and renewal. Remind

her that she can continue on during

rough weather,

holding on to the rainbow of hope

found in Christ Jesus.

For to this we labor and strive, that we
have put our hope in the living God, who
is the Savior of all men, and especially of
those who believe. Command and teach
these things.   _1 Timothy 4:10–11_

*U*nderstand

your daughter, and build on her

God-given talents and strengths.

Have realistic expectations for her

rather than comparing her with

the girl down the street or a sibling.

There are different kinds of gifts,
but the same Spirit. There are different
kinds of service, but the same Lord.
There are different kinds of working, but
the same God works all of them in all men.

1 Corinthians 12:4–6

alues

are a lifelong conversation.

Talk openly about your Christian

values as well as your family's standards.

I urge you to live a life worthy
of the calling you have received.

Ephesians 4:1

Wait

patiently for your daughter to fully

mature into a Christian woman.

God's time is not always our time, and

each child develops at a varying pace.

But do not forget this one thing, dear friends:
With the Lord a day is like a thousand years,
and a thousand years are like a day.

2 Peter 3:8

EXamine

your attitude when you begin

to feel negative toward your daughter.

Sometimes mothers and daughters have

differences that cannot be resolved, and

one of them needs to be the bigger

person. Ask God to help you overlook

differences during these times.

So in everything, do to others what you would
have them do to you, for this sums up
the Law and the Prophets.   *Matthew 7:12*

Your daughter is your own, and no one has written a script for her. God gives you a learning laboratory—your home —to start over every day. With God's grace, you can begin anew.

Then little children were brought to Jesus for Him to place His hands on them and pray for them. But the disciples rebuked those who brought them. Jesus said, "Let the little children come to Me, and do not hinder them, for the kingdom of heaven belongs to such as these." *Matthew 19:13–14*

Zealously

celebrate each day

as an opportunity to share God's love

with your daughter. Talk about God

being revealed in your

daily activities, and ask her

to look for the same in her life.

This is the day the LORD has made;
let us rejoice and be glad in it.

Psalm 118:24